NEW YORK TIMES BESTSELLING AUTHOR
KAILYN LOWRY'S

HUSTLE

& Heart

ADULT COLORING BOOK

T0089281

A POST HILL PRESS BOOK

Kailyn Lowry's Hustle and Heart Adult Coloring Book
© 2016 by Kailyn Lowry
All Rights Reserved

ISBN: 978-1-68261-164-7

Interior layout by Greg Johnson, Textbook Perfect

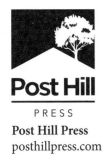

Post Hill
PRESS
Post Hill Press
posthillpress.com

Printed in the United States of America

FOLLOW YOUR HEART,
BUT
WATCH YOUR STEP.

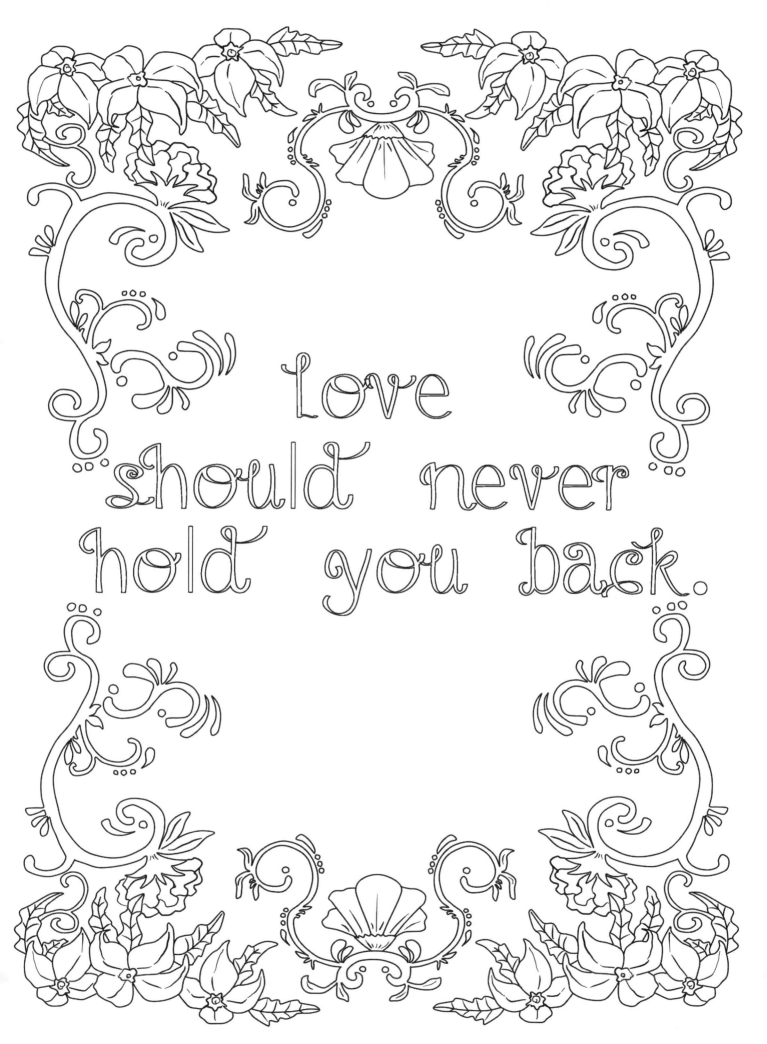

Love should never hold you back.

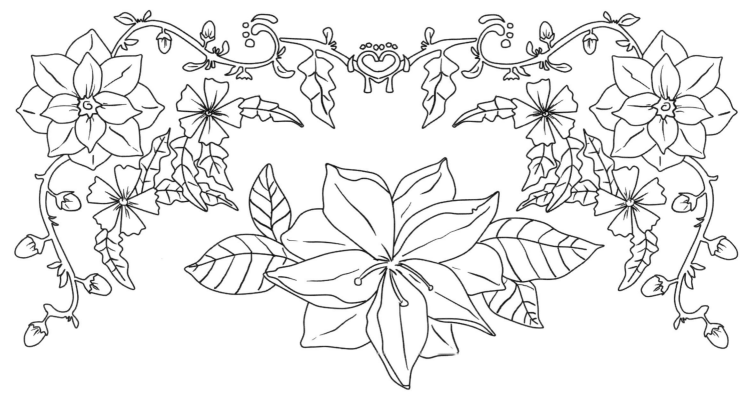

Loving yourself
is a superpower.

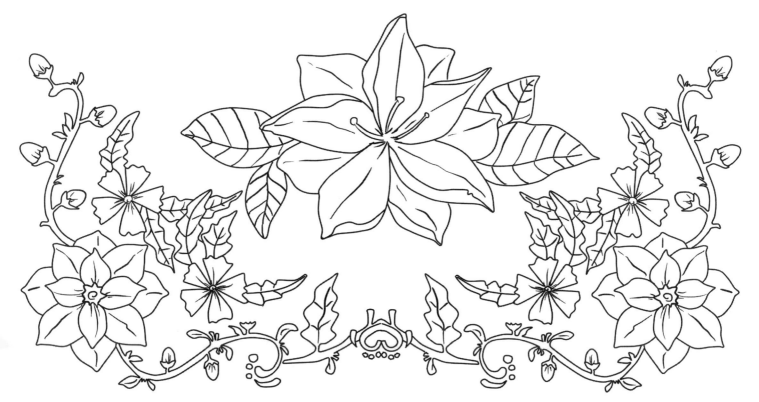

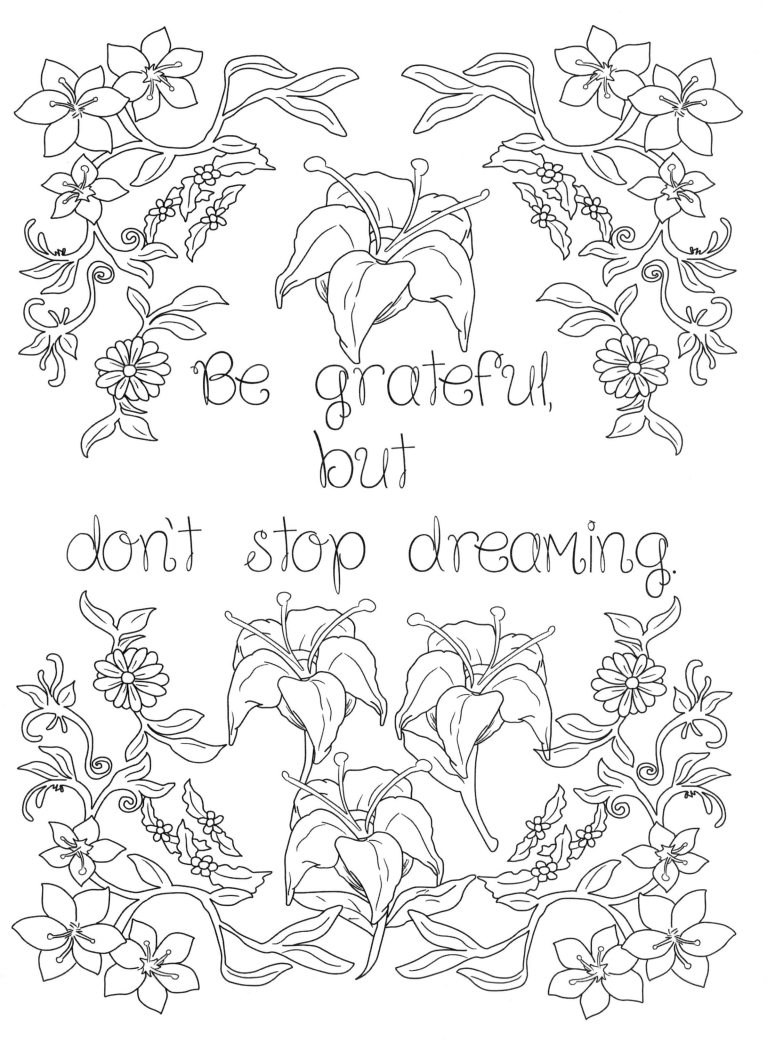

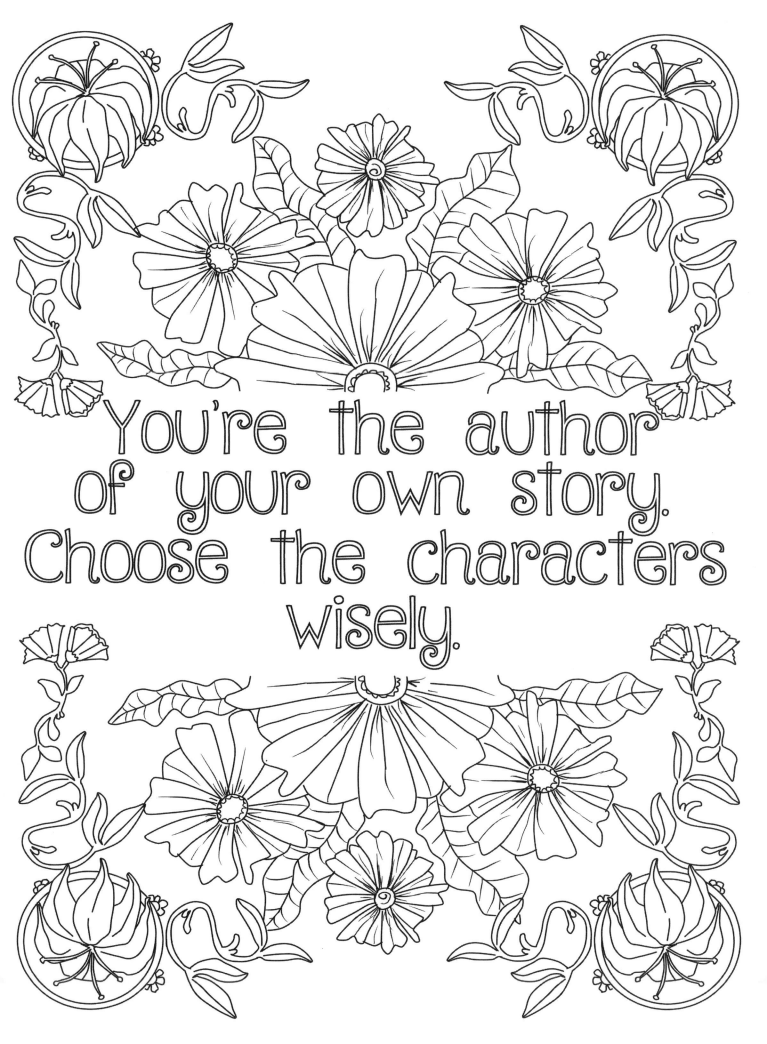

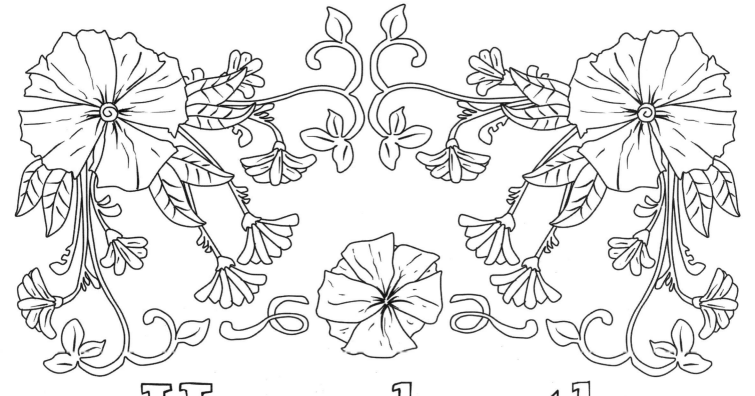

Have hustle and have heart.

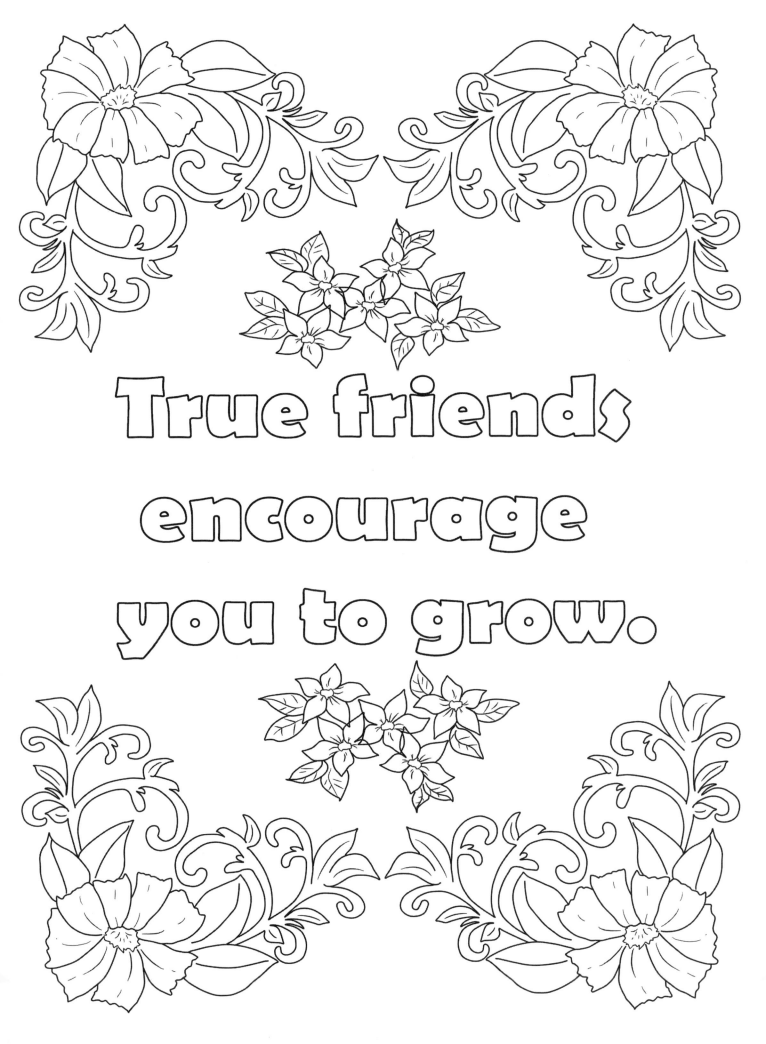

True friends encourage you to grow.

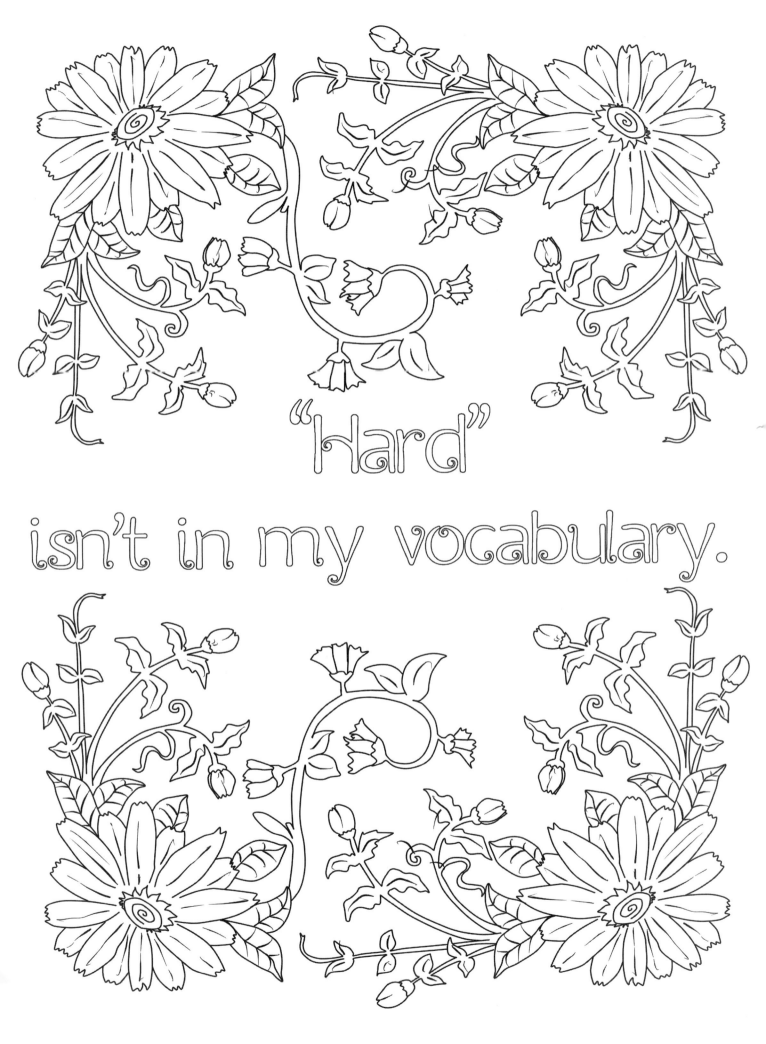

"Hard"

isn't in my vocabulary.

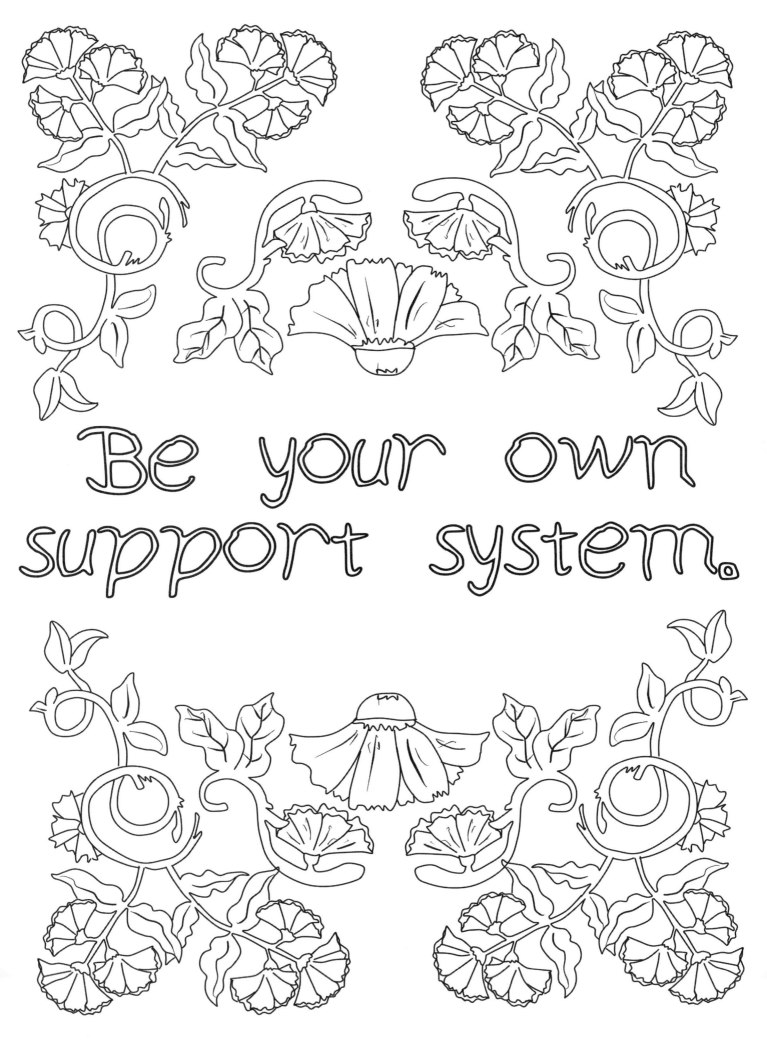

Be your own support system.

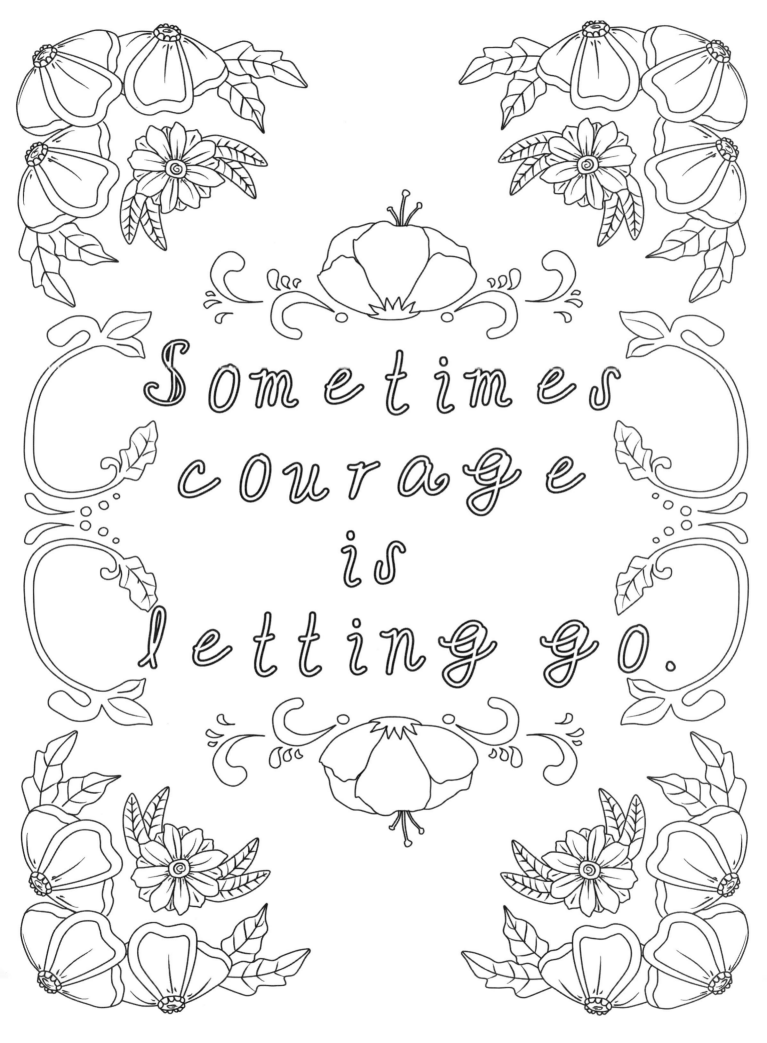

Sometimes courage is letting go.

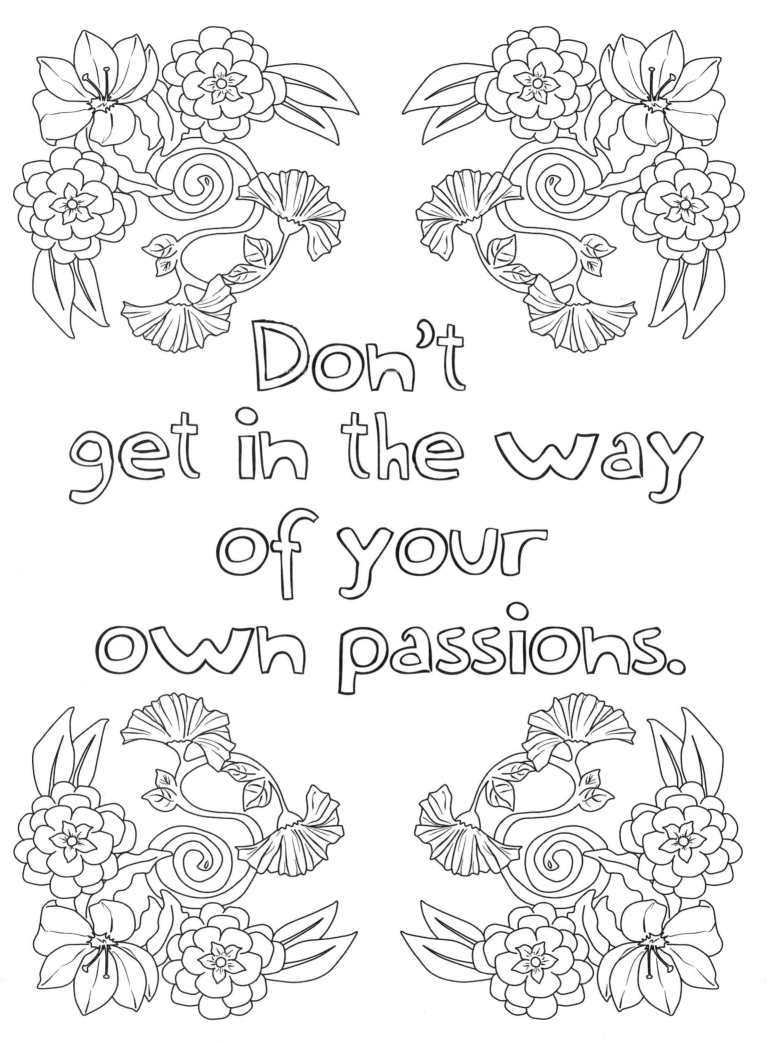

Don't get in the way of your own passions.

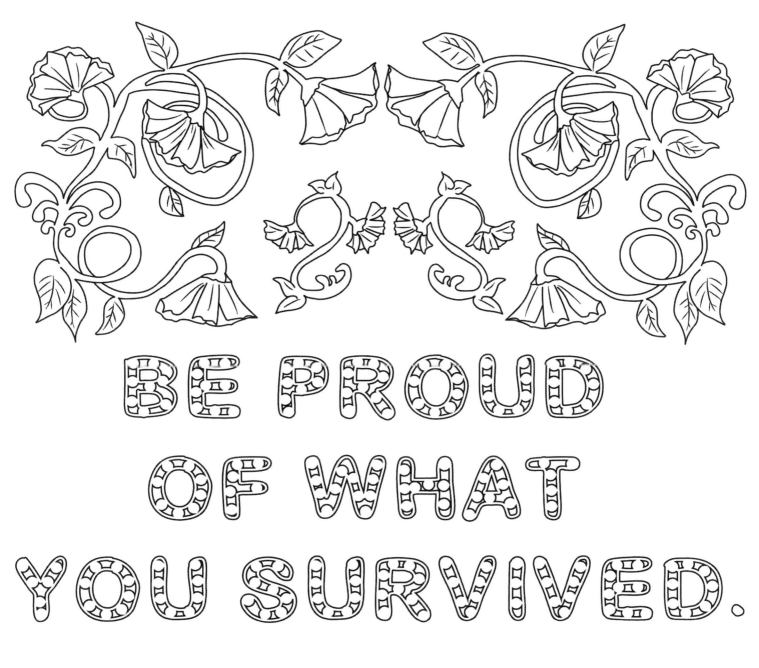

BE PROUD OF WHAT YOU SURVIVED.

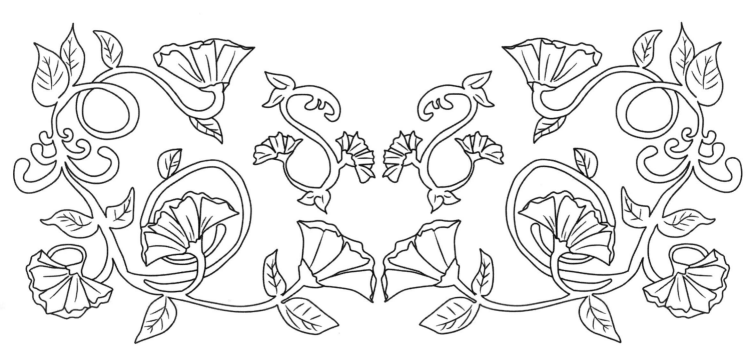

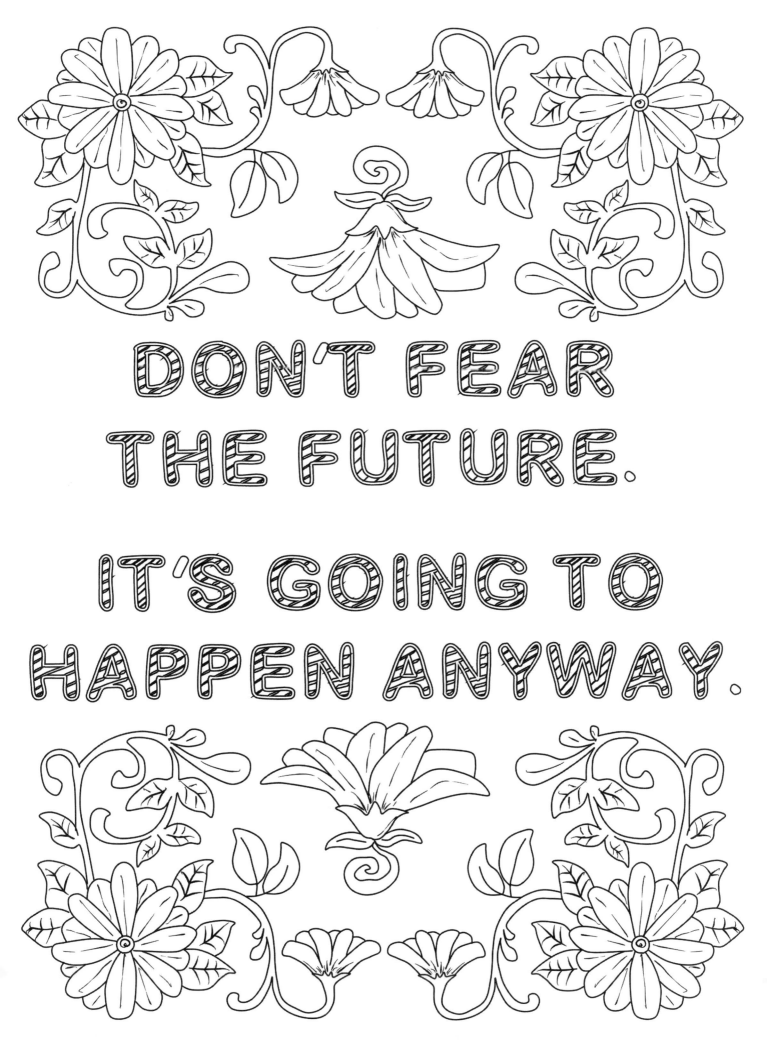

DON'T FEAR THE FUTURE.

IT'S GOING TO HAPPEN ANYWAY.

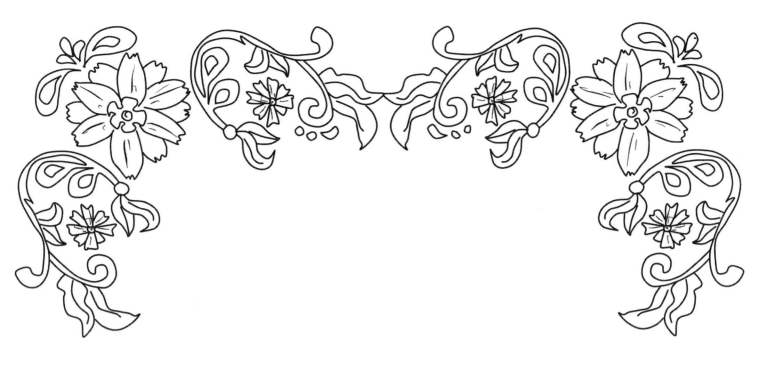

THE KINDNESS
OF STRANGERS
IS AN AMAZING THING.

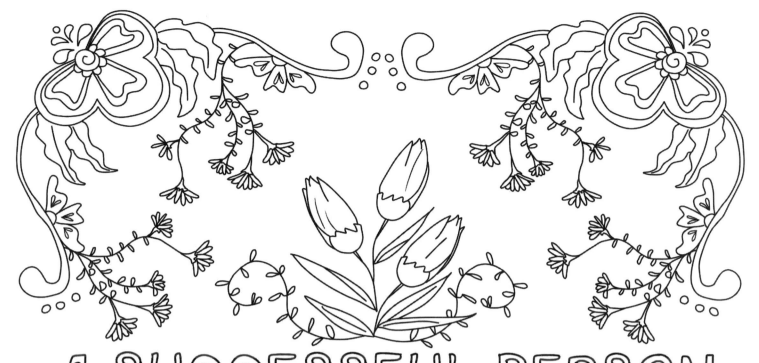

A SUCCESSFUL PERSON
IS ONE WHO CAN
BUILD A FOUNDATION
WITH THE BRICKS
THAT HAVE BEEN
THROWN AT THEM.

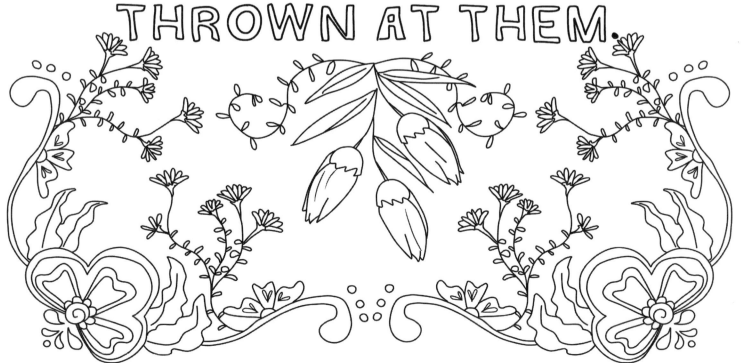

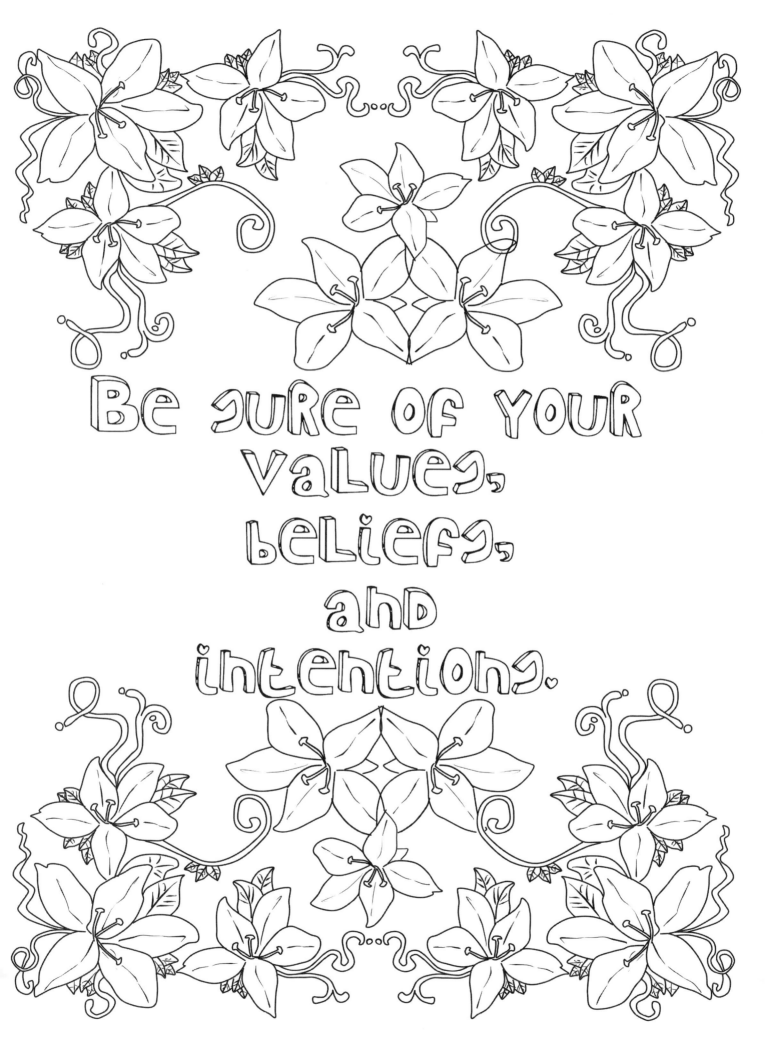

Be sure of your values, beliefs, and intentions.

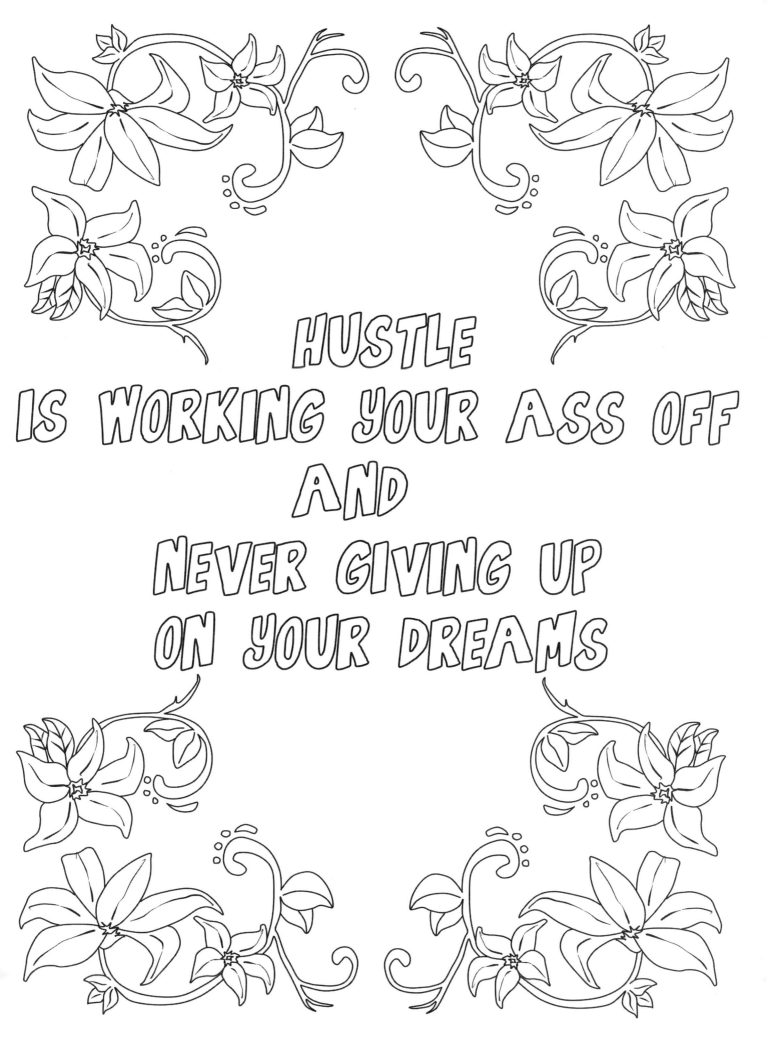

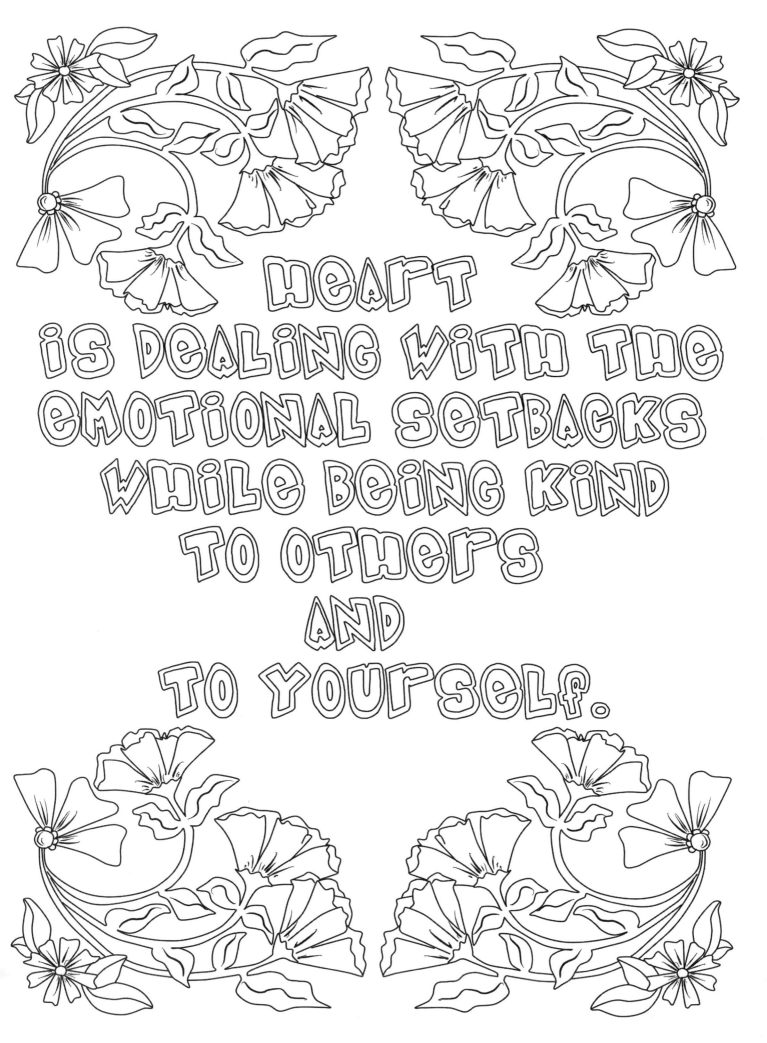

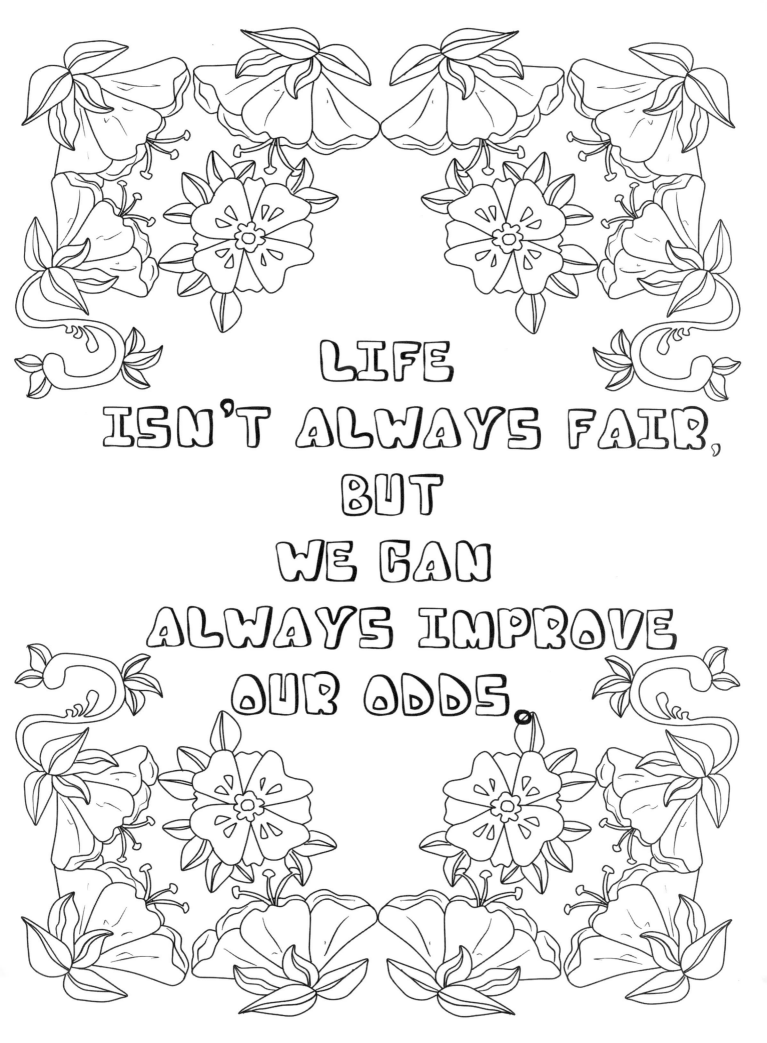

LIFE
ISN'T ALWAYS FAIR,
BUT
WE CAN
ALWAYS IMPROVE
OUR ODDS.

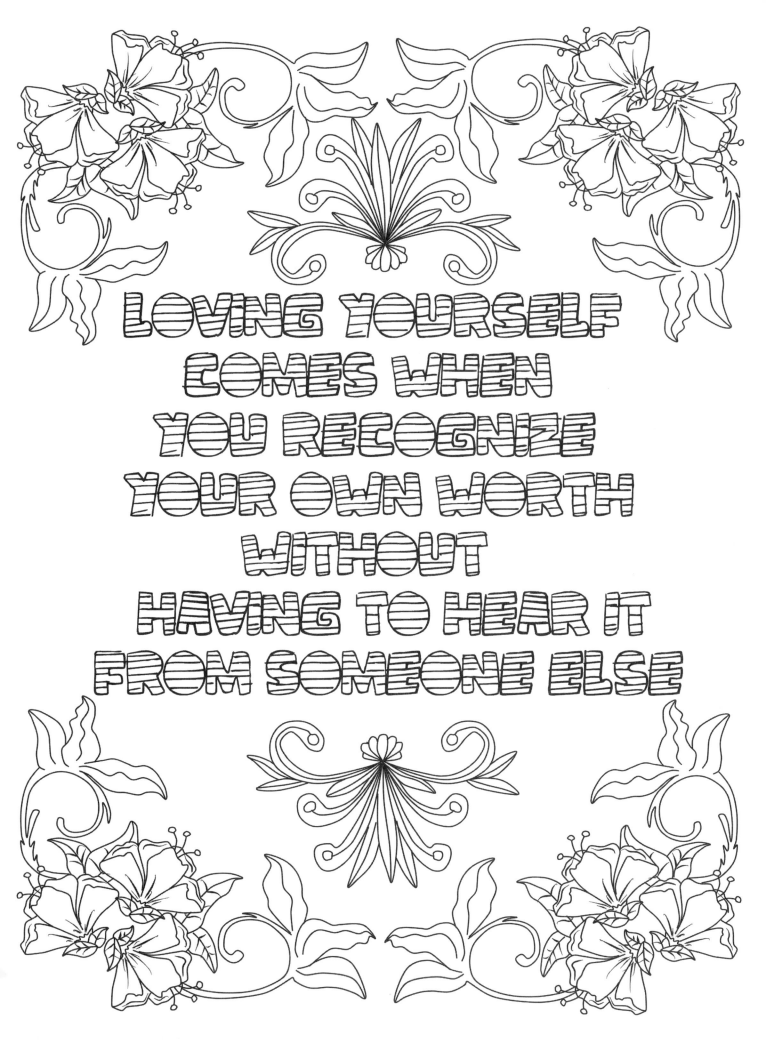

LOVING YOURSELF COMES WHEN YOU RECOGNIZE YOUR OWN WORTH WITHOUT HAVING TO HEAR IT FROM SOMEONE ELSE

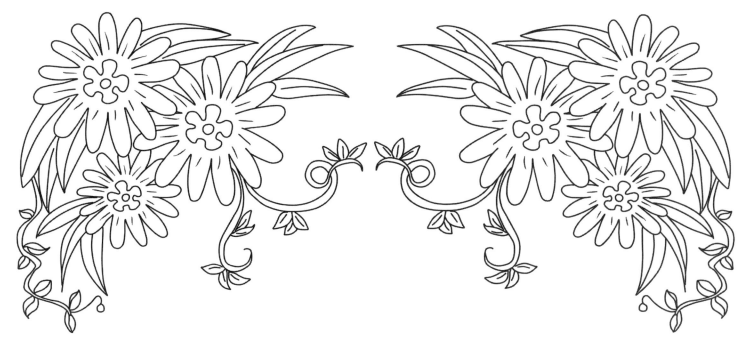

Pleasure and pain come naturally.

Gratitude takes practice.

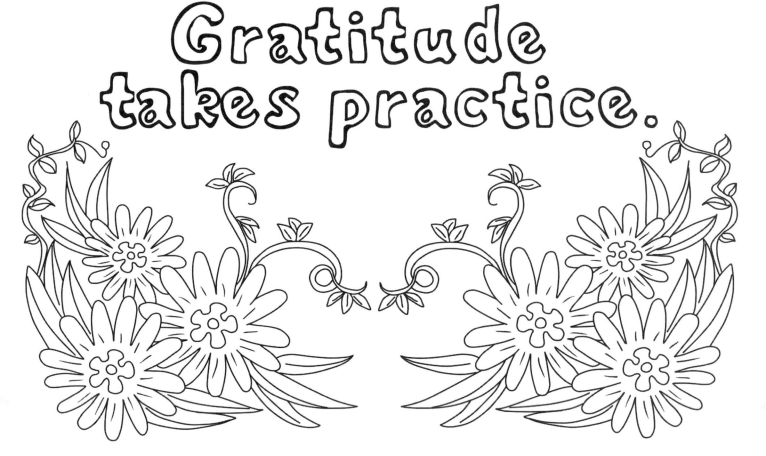

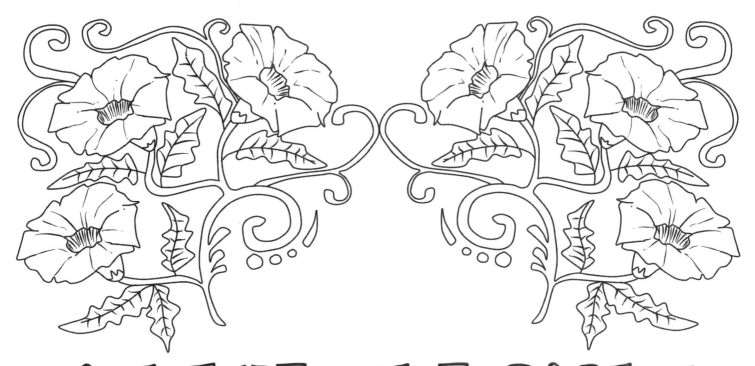

i HAVE THE RiGHT
TO DECiDE
WHAT KiND OF
PERSON
i WANT TO BE.

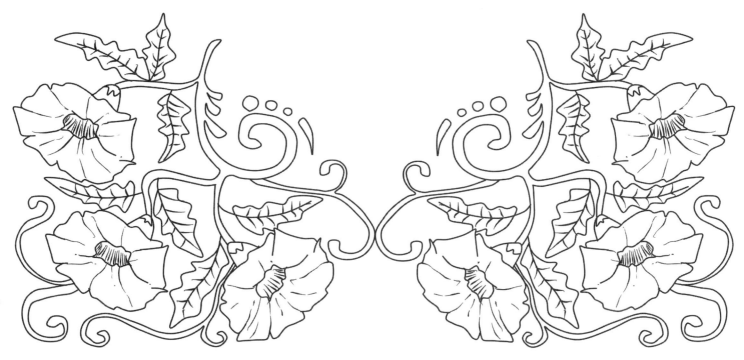

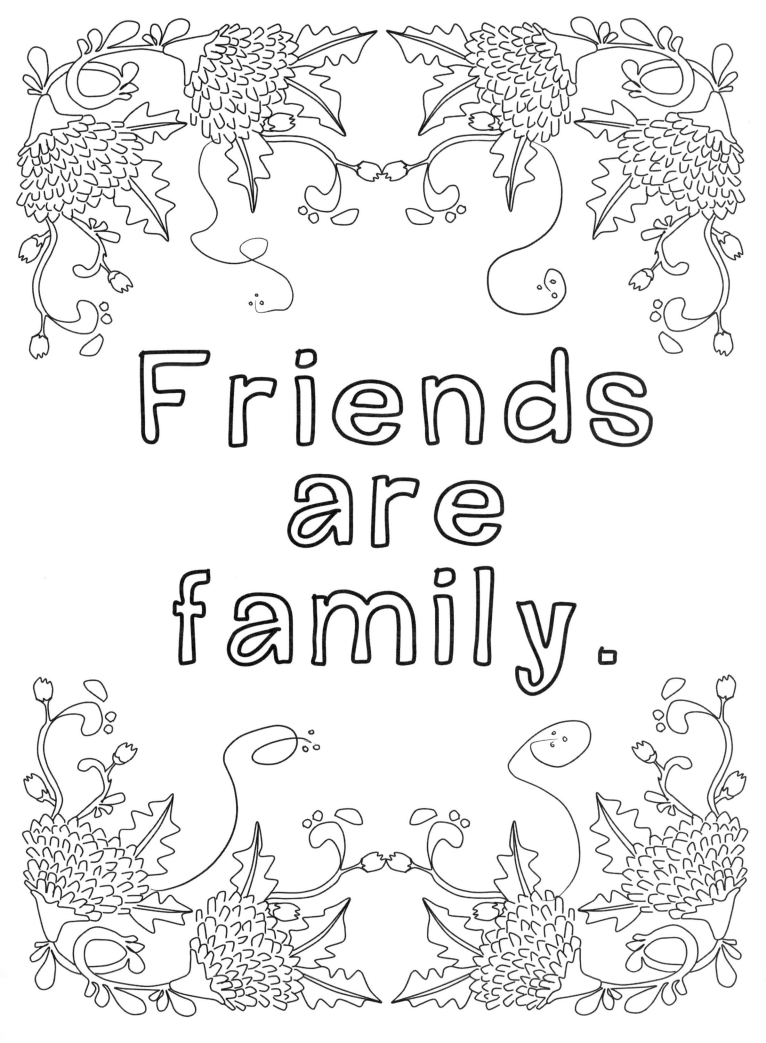

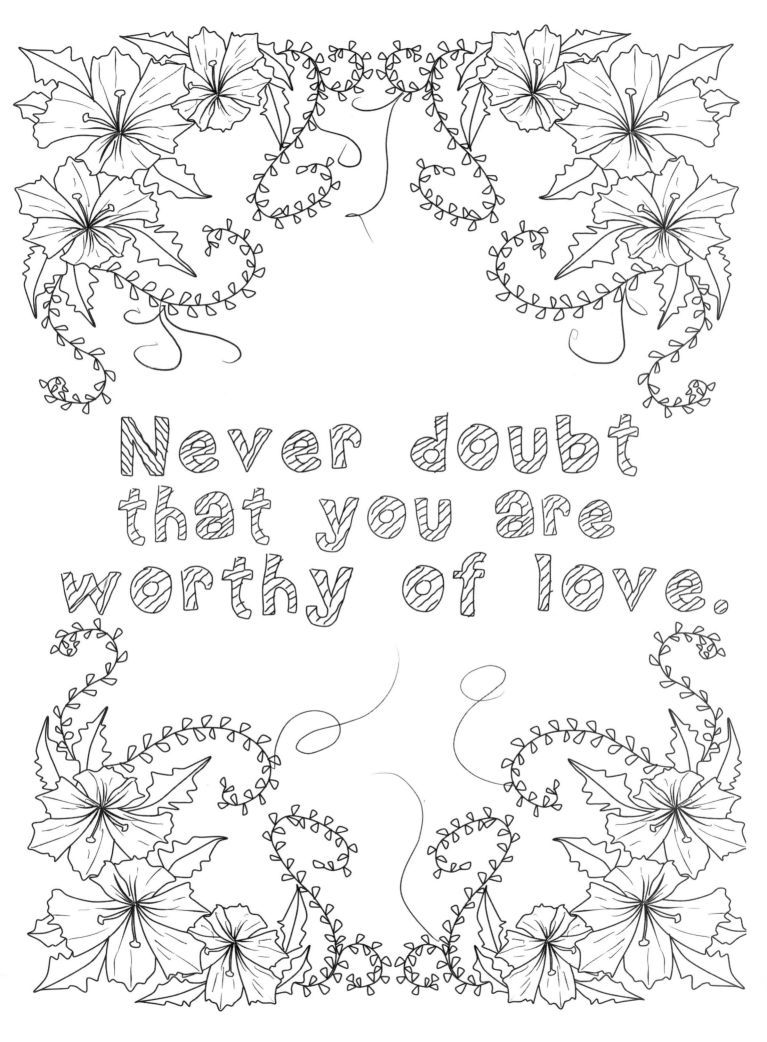

Never doubt
that you are
worthy of love.

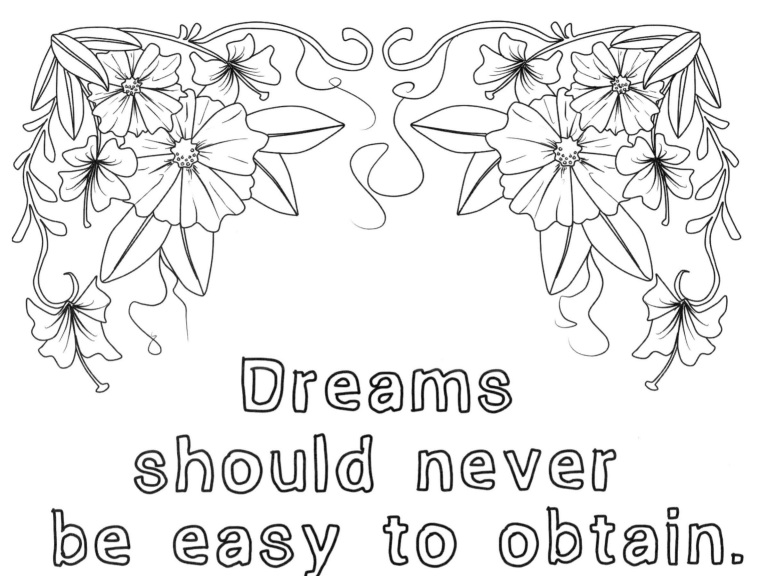

Dreams should never be easy to obtain.

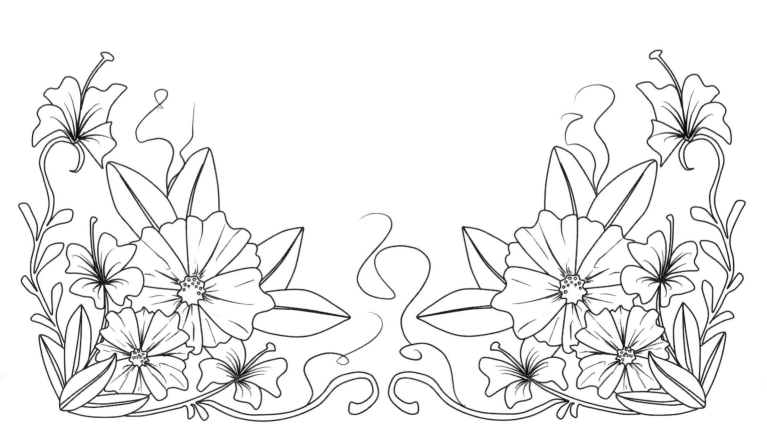

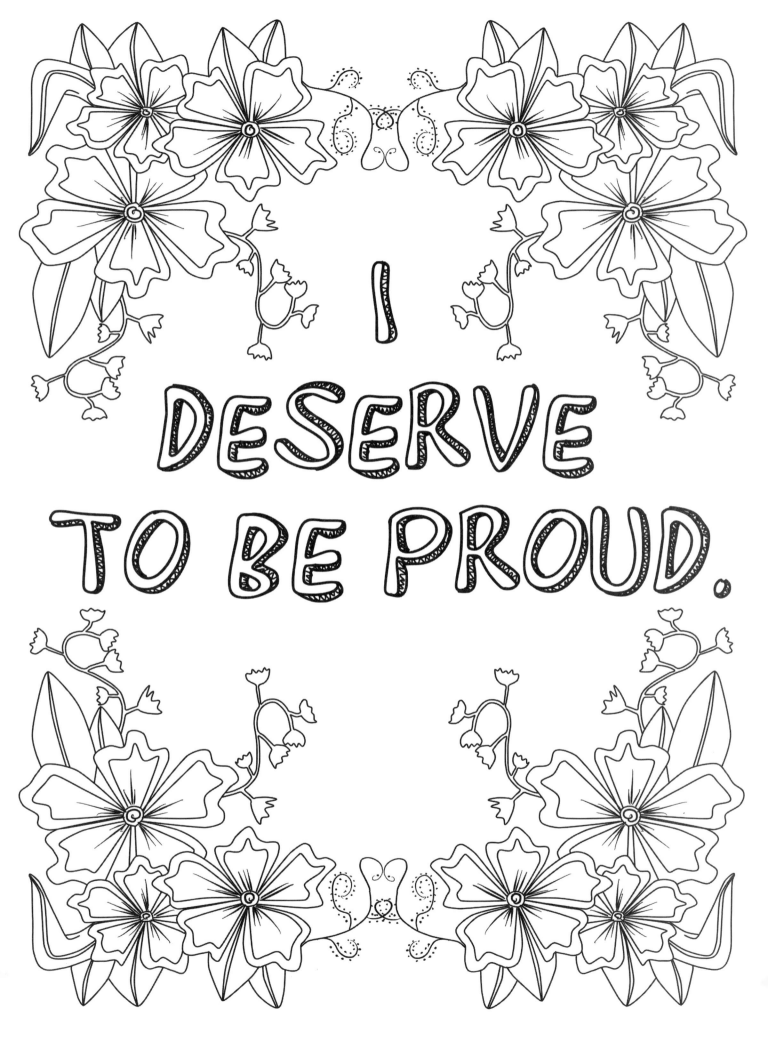

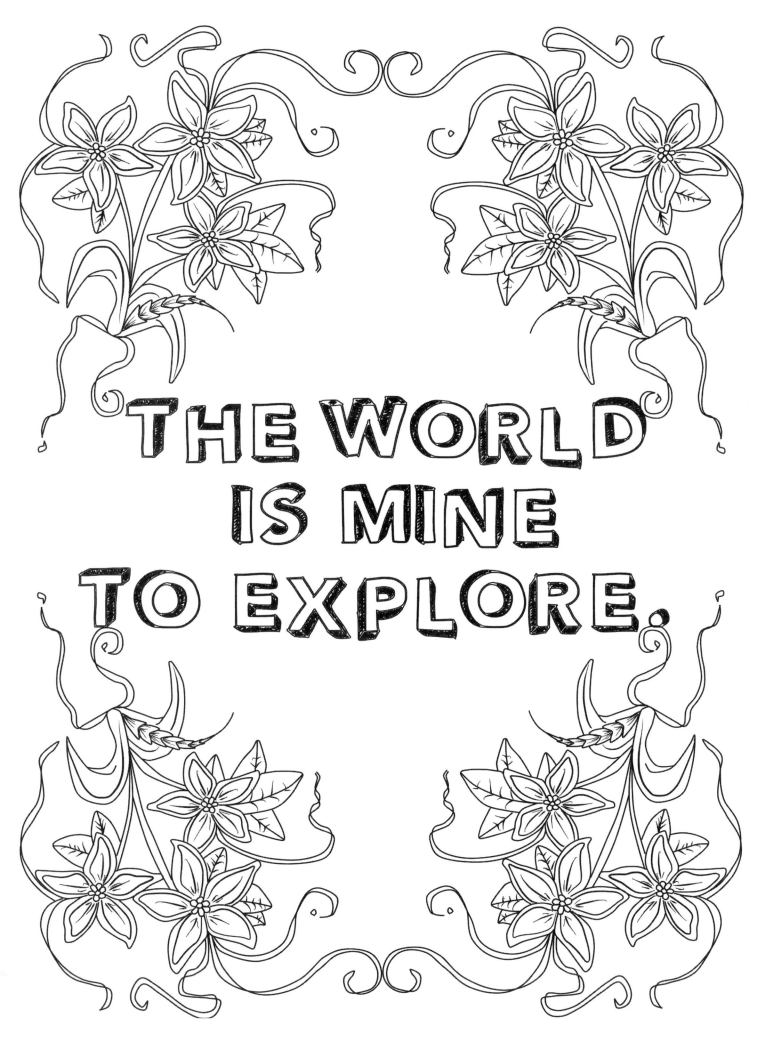

THE WORLD
IS MINE
TO EXPLORE.

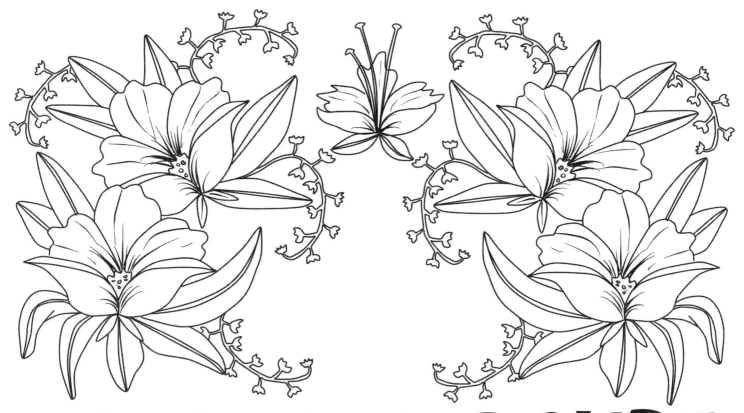

NEVER EVER DOUBT HOW MUCH I BELIEVE IN YOU.

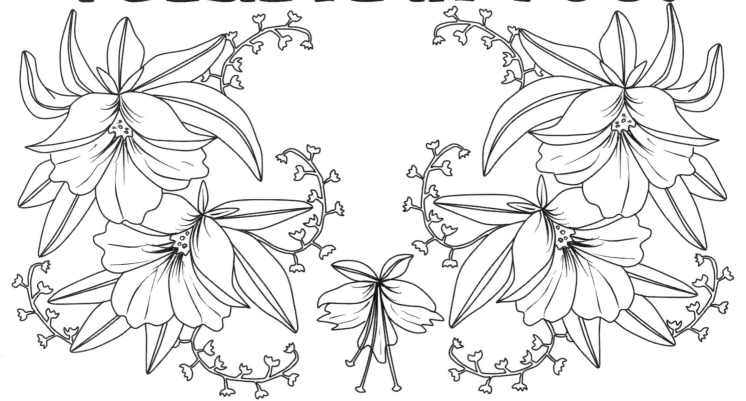

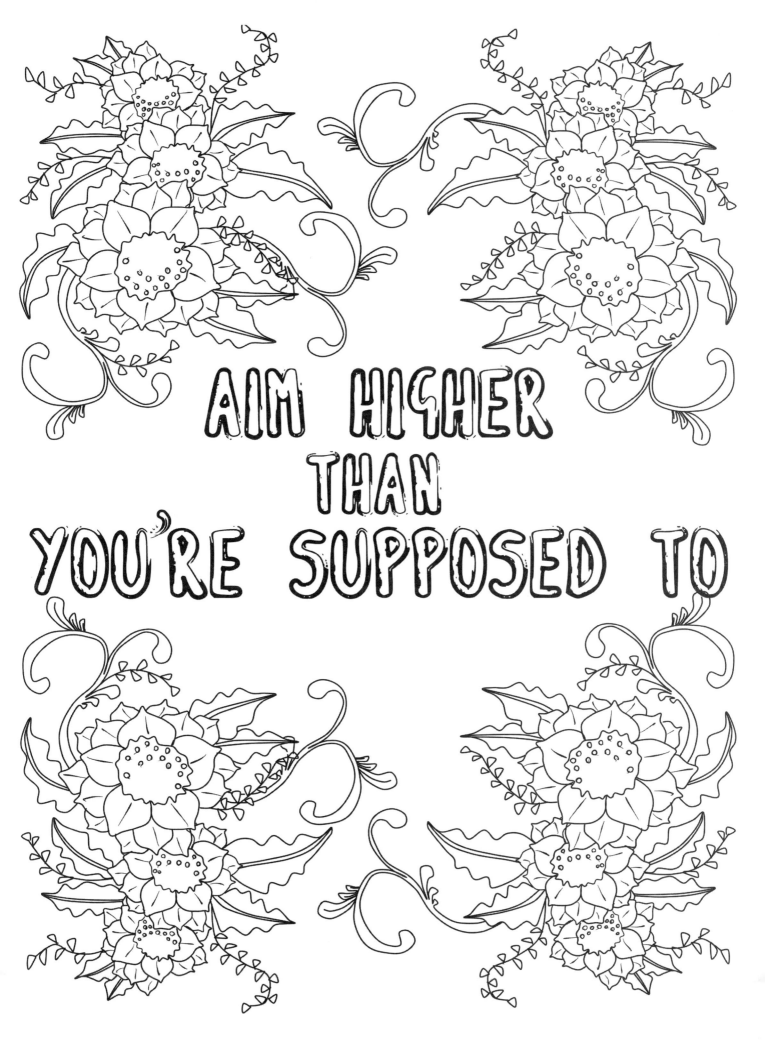

AIM HIGHER
THAN
YOU'RE SUPPOSED TO

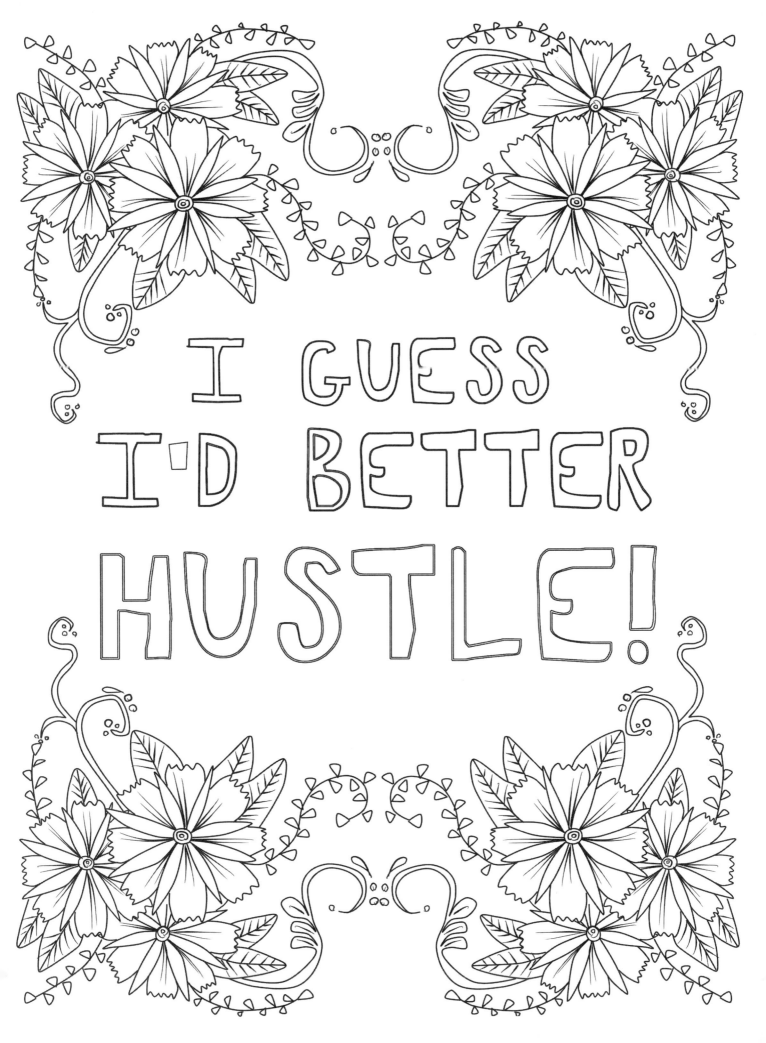

Also Available from *Kailyn Lowry*

Hustle and Heart

As a small-town girl turned Teen Mom, bestselling author and social media celebrity, Kailyn Lowry has been through many ups and downs. Now, she's sharing the inspiration that got her through it all. From bullying, sexual assault and body image issues to motherhood, marriage and career challenges, Kailyn wants you to know that there's nothing you can't survive with a little bit of hustle and heart.

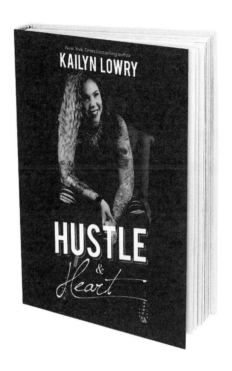

EAN 9781618688156
Price: $15.00

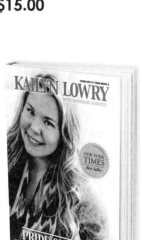

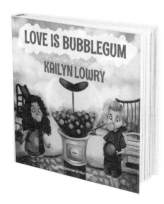

Pride Over Pity
EAN 9781682612842
Price: $14.00

Love is Bubblegum
EAN 9781618688606
Price: $17.99

Available wherever books are sold.

Post Hill
PRESS